Tito Puente

by Mary Olmstead

Chicago, Illinois

© 2005 Raintree
Published by Raintree, a division of Reed Elsevier, Inc.
Chicago, Illinois
Customer Service: 888-363-4266
Visit our website at www.raintreelibrary.com

For information, address the publisher
Raintree, 100 N. LaSalle, Suite 1200, Chicago, IL 60602

Photo research by Scott Braut
Printed and bound in China by South China Printing
    Co. Ltd.

09 08 07 06 05
10 9 8 7 6 5 4 3 2 1

Library of Congress Cataloging-in-Publication Data
    Olmstead, Mary.
    Tito Puente / Mary Olmstead.
      p. cm. -- (Hispanic-American biographies)
    Summary: A biography of band leader and recording
artist who grew up in
Spanish Harlem and gained worldwide popularity as the
"King of Latin
Music."
    Includes bibliographical references (p.   ) and index.
      ISBN 1-4109-0713-9 (library binding-hardcover) --
ISBN 1-4109-0919-0 (paperback)
    1. Puente, Tito, 1923---Juvenile literature. 2.
Musicians--Latin
America--Biography--Juvenile literature. [1. Puente, Tito,
1923- 2.
Musicians. 3. Hispanic Americans--Biography.] I. Title.
II. Series:
Olmstead, Mary. Hispanic-American biographies.
    ML3930.P83O5 2004
    784.4'81888'092--dc21

                            2003021650

Acknowledgments
The publisher would like to thank the following for permission to reproduce photographs:
p. 4 Guy Le Querrec/Magnum Photos; pp. 6, 23, 32 Hulton Archive/Getty Images; pp. 8, 14, 24 Bettmann/Corbis; p. 16 Underwood & Underwood/Corbis; pp. 20, 38, 46 Martin Cohen/congahead.com; p. 26 Widener Je/ Corbis Sygma; p. 29 Corbis; p. 31 Alton Taube, courtesy The Juilliard School; p. 36 Bob Parent Photo Archive; p. 37 courtesy Universal Records p. 40 Michael Caulfield/Reuters Photo Archive/NewsCom; p. 44 Suzanne Plunkett/AP Wide World Photo; p. 45 Reuters NewMedia Inc./Corbis; p. 48 Roger Ressmeyer/Corbis; pp. 52, 57 Mike Blake/Reuters Photo Archive/NewsCom; pp. 54, 59 Kevork Djansezian/AP Wide World Photos

Cover photograph by Frank Driggs Collection/Archive Photos/Hulton Archive/Getty Images

Every effort has been made to contact copyright holders of any material reproduced in this book. Any omissions will be rectified in subsequent printings if notice is given to the publisher.

Some words are shown in bold, like this. You can find out what they mean by looking in the glossary.

Contents

Tito Puente was one of the greatest bandleaders of all time. He introduced Latin jazz to millions of listeners.

Introduction

Tito Puente wrote, played, and **conducted** music for over fifty years. He played drums with lightning speed that set a new standard for other **percussionists.** He could direct his band and play drums at the same time. Without missing a beat, he snapped his head and waved his drumsticks to lead the band. He was amazing to watch, and the music he played was fun to dance to.

Tito Puente used elements from both **Latin** and **jazz** music to play a new kind of music called **Latin jazz.** Latin music is a broad term for music that comes from Latin America. It also means any music influenced by Latin sounds. Jazz is a form of music developed by African-American musicians in the early 1900s. The music has a strong **rhythm** and features **solos** and **improvisation.** Improvisation is music made up on the spot.

Tito Puente was often very expressive while he played the drums.

Tito Puente wrote and published over four hundred original songs. He also adapted more than 2,000 songs written by other people, giving their songs a Latin beat. He is best known for *Dance Mania*, an all-time best selling album released in 1958. The hard-working bandleader recorded more than 100 albums.

Tito Puente was wildly popular with listeners all over America during the 1950s. His performances dazzled audiences who called him *El Rey del* **Mambo**, which is Spanish for "The King of the Mambo." The mambo is a type of **Latin music** that Tito helped make popular in the 1950s. Sometimes Tito was simply called *El Rey*, or "The King." Today, a whole new generation has discovered Latin music. Tito Puente's influence can still be heard in these songs that are popular around the world.

Tito Puente loved to share the joy of music with others. As a bandleader, he presented the talents of other musicians. He introduced listeners to female Latin singers. He established a scholarship fund to encourage younger artists to study music. Almost to the end of his life, he played between 200 and 300 shows a year. Music was indeed Tito Puente's life.

This photo from the 1940s shows the Harlem neighborhood in New York City.

Chapter 1:
The Early Years

E rnest Anthony Puente Jr. was born April 20, 1923, at Harlem Hospital in New York City. He was nicknamed Ernestito (Spanish for "little Ernest") when he was young. From *Ernestito* came the shortened name *Tito,* which is what he was called the rest of his life.

Tito's parents, Ernesto Sr. and Ercila Puente, moved to New York City from the Caribbean island of Puerto Rico shortly before Tito was born. Like many Puerto Ricans, the Puentes moved to the United States in search of opportunity. In New York, Tito's father Ernest found work as a foreman in a razor blade factory. A foreman is the person who watches over the other workers. Tito's sister Anna was born in 1926. A brother named Alberto was born a few years later. Sadly, Alberto died after falling from a fire escape when he was only four.

Spanish Harlem

Tito grew up in a New York City neighborhood called Harlem. The part of Harlem where Tito lived was known both as Spanish Harlem and *El Barrio.* The neighborhood was a mix of different **ethnic** groups who spoke different languages. The ethnic groups living in Harlem were constantly changing. When Tito was young, there were mostly Italians, Jews, Puerto Ricans, Cubans, and African Americans living in the neighborhood.

Neighborhood schools in Spanish Harlem were **integrated**— children of all races and ethnic groups went there. Tito's parents made sure their children learned about their own Puerto Rican background. The family prepared foods that were typical of Puerto Rico. Ernest and Ercila insisted that the children speak and read Spanish, the language of Puerto Rico. This meant that Tito was **bilingual** because he could speak both English and Spanish.

When Tito was growing up, **discrimination** was common against people of color. In some places, Hispanics and African Americans could not eat in the same restaurants or go to the same schools as whites. Some Puerto Ricans are very dark skinned, and some are not. Light-skinned Tito did not suffer the effects of discrimination as much as he would have if he had been darker.

Life in Spanish Harlem had its problems, but it was also different from many other areas of the United States. By the time

Latinos in Spanish Harlem

Puerto Rico became a possession of the United States after the Spanish-American War of 1898. Puerto Ricans could not vote in national elections, but they were granted most other rights of United States citizens in 1917. Shortly afterwards, Puerto Ricans began to migrate to the United States in large numbers. They came to take advantage of the opportunities that were not available in Puerto Rico.

Many **Latinos** settled in Harlem. Harlem is a section of New York City located on the island of Manhattan. Many African Americans lived there. Latinos came to Harlem partly for the same reasons African Americans did—for job opportunities and the rich **cultural** life in Harlem. Tito's parents encouraged their children to take advantage of the many cultural opportunities to be found in Harlem.

The east part of Harlem was known as Spanish Harlem. It got that name because of the large number of Latinos who lived there. A Latino is a person from Latin America or one whose ancestors came from Latin America. The neighborhood was also called *El Barrio.* A *barrio* is a Spanish-speaking neighborhood in a city or town.

Tito was born, **discrimination** was not as widespread in Spanish Harlem as it was in the American South. In the 1910s, African Americans had come from all over the country to live in Harlem. They helped spread the idea that the **culture** of black people was something that they should be proud of. Living among people of different races and **ethnic** backgrounds made everyone more accepting of each other.

Tito described his neighborhood as "pretty rough." His family was poor. They moved often because they were always looking for a cheaper place to rent. "Sometimes I'd come from school and I'd find out that they had moved across the street because they gave them two months' rent [for free]," he remembered.

The Young Musician

When he was growing up, Tito liked doing the typical things other kids his age did. He played baseball with his friends. He rode his bicycle around the neighborhood. He joined the Boy Scouts.

In 1930, when he was seven, Tito's mother enrolled him in piano lessons at the nearby New York School of Music. Tito's piano teacher soon discovered the young boy had natural musical ability. Tito also studied piano on occasion with famous Latin American **composers** and musicians. The family did not have much money. But Tito's mother found a way to pay for lessons.

Tito took piano lessons for seven years. He also began taking drum lessons somewhere between the ages of ten and twelve. The young musician learned the basics of drumming from a teacher named Mr. Williams. At home, Tito used forks and spoons or whatever was at hand to create the **rhythms** he heard in his head. He drummed on the furniture, on the table, on anything that made noise. "I was always banging on boxes, on the window sill," admitted Tito as an adult.

Stars of the Future

When Tito was about twelve, he and his younger sister Anna enjoyed watching the movies of Fred Astaire and Ginger Rogers. They were popular stars who danced together in several 1930s movies. Their mother noticed her children's interest in dance and signed them up for lessons. The dance lessons would pay off for years to come. Tito became one of the few bandleaders of his time who really knew how to dance.

Tito and Anna joined a neighborhood organization for children interested in performing. It was called the Stars of the Future. The organization met at the church their family attended. Every year, the Stars of the Future recognized children's achievements as performing artists. The most talented children were crowned king or queen for their artistic ability and popularity as performers. Tito was such a good dancer that he was crowned king four times.

C-1939-123

Jazz musician Count Basie was one of Tito Puente's early musical influences. Basie made some of the most exciting big band records ever recorded. This is a picture of Basie in the film Made in Paris.

Chapter 2:
A Musical Feast

Tito was surrounded with music as he was growing up. New York City offered some of the best music in the country. There was **Latin music.** There were great **jazz** artists and big bands that played a new music called **swing.** Tito heard popular dance bands play live on the radio. Sometimes he and his father went to local theaters like the Paramount and the Strand to see jazz bands live.

The great jazz artists of the time influenced Tito. He counted Duke Ellington and Count Basie as two of his musical heroes. Tito listened to their records and the records of other popular jazz artists—Woody Herman, Dizzy Gillespie, and Charlie Parker.

Jazz drummer Gene Krupa was another one of Tito's heroes. He loved Krupa's drum **solo** on "Sing, Sing, Sing," a popular song at that time. Tito memorized the drum solo—that part of a song where one instrument gets to play by itself—note for note. He won a drum contest playing it.

Bandleader Xavier Cugat's showy performances influenced Tito Puente to put on a great show when he became a bandleader.

A Mix of Styles

Tito also loved **Latin music.** As a teen, he heard the popular Latin big band music of Xavier Cugat. Cugat was a Spanish bandleader and violinist who grew up in Cuba. He moved to New York City in 1915. In the 1930s, he formed a popular band.

Part of the band's appeal was the great show they put on. All the musicians wore flashy red jackets. Dancers with the band demonstrated the latest Latin-American dance steps. They encouraged audiences to follow and learn. The band had a singer, and Cugat played the violin. In between songs, he would continue to entertain by talking to the audience and band members.

The biggest appeal of Cugat's band was the music itself. People all over the country listened to his music on the radio. Cugat's musicians played a variety of **percussion** instruments. They played maracas (rattles that are shaken), bongos (small pairs of connected drums played with the hands), and congas (tall drums played with the hands).

Cugat and other **Latin** musicians used percussion in their bands to create interesting side **rhythms** that supported the main rhythm in unexpected ways. Audiences everywhere were hooked on the lively sounds that played off each other. Years later as a bandleader, Tito would also give audiences what they came for— great music and a good show.

When he was in his early teens, Tito and his father often listened to the **Latin music** being played in the clubs and on the streets of their own neighborhood. Musicians from Puerto Rico and Cuba freely shared their musical traditions with each other. Sometimes they added **jazz** elements to their music to produce a new sound.

The result was an interesting blend of Latin **percussion** combined with jazz-like melodies. Percussion players took turns departing from the main **rhythm** at different times during a song. This created rich layers of sound. People came to listen and dance to the music.

Cuban Influences on Tito's Music: Mario Bauzá and "Machito" Frank Grillo

Two important influences on Tito Puente were Cubans "Machito" Frank Grillo (1909–1984) and his friend and brother-in-law Mario Bauzá (1911–1993). Both moved to New York City in the 1930s.

Bauzá was important in jazz history. He discovered jazz singer Ella Fitzgerald and introduced Dizzy Gillespie to other jazz musicians.

Duke Ellington and Count Basie also asked Bauzá to join their bands. Instead, Bauzá became musical director for the Machito Orchestra. Bauzá helped promote musicians whose talent he admired, including young Tito Puente. Bauzá is often credited with inventing **Latin jazz.**

The Teen Years

By 1937, music was the main focus of Tito's life. In high school, the fourteen-year-old could be found playing piano in the auditorium during lunch. A crowd usually gathered to watch him play. In between classes, Tito and a few friends would sing in the stairway. After school, they sang on street corners.

Tito met Frank Grillo, who was nicknamed Machito, through other musicians he knew. The singer and trumpet player had come from Cuba in 1937. On weekends, Tito played with Machito and other musicians in the neighborhood at 110th Street and Fifth Avenue near Park Plaza.

Machito encouraged Tito's musical ability. Tito learned a lot from playing piano and saxophone with Machito and the other street musicians who showed up at these informal sessions. He watched as Cuban musicians played timbales—two small, metal kettledrums on a stand played with drumsticks.

To Tito, it seemed natural to mix different styles of music because that is what he heard in Spanish Harlem. He began to experiment with making new **arrangements** of songs he heard. That means he took a piece of music and adapted it for different types of instruments or styles of music.

Tito Puente performs with "Machito" Frank Grillo in New York City.

Swing and Big Bands

In the 1930s a musical style called **swing** appeared. Swing is a simpler form of jazz that has a loose, flowing **rhythm.** The beat of swing music is lively and easy to dance to. The music soon became very popular.

Swing was played by big bands that had three or four each of saxophones, trumpets, and trombones. They also had drums, piano, string bass, and guitar. Big bands were larger than the small jazz bands that played in the 1920s. Some famous bandleaders were Duke Ellington, Glenn Miller, Tommy Dorsey, and Benny Goodman.

During World War II (1939–1945), jazz and swing were seen as symbols of home for American soldiers. Both the United States Army and the Navy formed military big bands. These bands followed the troops and played music as a way to help soldiers forget, at least for a while, the horrors of war.

A Big Step

By the late 1930s, Cuban music and **swing** music were very popular. It was easy for musicians to find work. In New York, many hotel ballrooms hired two separate bands to play each night. One played Cuban music and the other played swing.

Tito dropped out of school in 1939 at sixteen to become a full-time musician. A few months later, he met a man named José Curbelo, a piano player who had just arrived from Cuba. Meeting Curbelo was a lucky break. The older musician was impressed with Tito's talent. Curbelo was offered a three-month job playing music in Miami. He invited Tito to go along.

Curbelo became Tito's mentor. A mentor is a person who shares his or her experience and knowledge with someone just starting out. Tito learned what it was like to tour as a professional musician. Curbelo taught Tito about the business side of music. He did not regret taking Tito to Miami. He said, "I thought I had seen the best drummers in Cuba . . . until I saw Tito perform."

Tito returned to New York at the end of the Miami tour. He found steady work playing in different bands. Two years later, he made his first recording with Vincent López's Suave **Swing** Orchestra. He made other recordings with Noro Morales's band. That band also made four short musical films. Movie musicals were very popular. Tito's musical career was off to a strong start.

This photograph of Vincent Lopez's band was taken on the beach at Atlantic City, New Jersey, in the 1930s.

Millions of men became soldiers and fought in World War II. Tito Puente became a soldier, too. During his time in the navy, he met other musicians.

Chapter 3: A Different Drummer

In June of 1942, the United States entered World War II. Young men everywhere were drafted, or called upon to serve their country. When the drummer for Machito's band was drafted, Machito hired Tito to take his place.

It was a lucky break for Tito to be able to work with his friend. Machito was blending Latin **rhythms** with **jazz** sounds—a musical style that would later be called **Latin jazz.** Machito's music director, Mario Bauzá, showed Tito how he created the musical **arrangements.**

At nineteen, Tito was developing his own performing style. He put together an interesting combination of **percussion** instruments. He chose timbales, a bass drum, and cymbals. The timbales allowed Tito to play drums standing up rather than sitting down like most drummers. This was unusual. It also gave Tito the freedom to move around.

Tito nearly always played standing up.

The placement of Tito's drum set was also unusual. It was placed in front of the orchestra, not towards the back or side. Audiences were better able to watch as well as listen to him play. What they saw was Tito's total concentration as his drumsticks moved with incredible speed. They saw his easy grin and humorous facial expressions.

Tito's speed was matched by his gracefulness. Years of childhood dance lessons gave the young showman a lightness of movement on stage. Audiences loved Tito's fancy footwork as he danced and played drums at the same time.

World War II (1939–1945)

A series of events led to the biggest war in history—World War II. The leaders of Germany, Italy, and Japan did not agree with the terms of peace drawn up after World War I ended in 1918. From 1931 to 1939, these countries took territories that did not belong to them.

World War II began on September 1, 1939, after Germany invaded Poland. Two days later, England and France demanded that Germany withdraw from Poland. Germany refused. England and France declared war on Germany. Within a week, other countries took sides.

Germany swept across Europe, crushing Poland, Denmark, Luxembourg, the Netherlands, Belgium, Norway, and France. Italy joined Germany's side. The fighting spread to Greece and northern Africa. Soon, battles were fought in nearly every part of the world.

On December 7, 1941, Japan bombed a United States military base in Pearl Harbor, Hawaii. The attack brought the United States into the war on the Allies' side. Countries supporting England and France were called the Allies. Supporters of Germany, Italy, and Japan were called the Axis powers. Thousands of United States citizens fought in the war. Like others his age, Tito Puente was drafted, or called into military service.

In Europe, the war ended on May 7, 1945, when Germany surrendered. On August 6 and August 9, the United States dropped the world's first atomic bombs on the Japanese cities of Hiroshima and Nagasaki. Japan surrendered on September 2, 1945.

The Navy Years

Tito's time with the Machito Orchestra was short because he was drafted that year, 1942, to serve in the United States Navy. He was assigned to the U.S.S. *Santee*. The ship escorted supply ships and passenger ships. Tito loaded ammunition into artillery (guns). He fought in nine battles that took place in the Atlantic and Pacific oceans. After the war, Tito received a presidential commendation for the part he played during combat.

Throughout his navy years, Tito continued to play music. He played drums and alto and tenor saxophones in a **swing** band on board ship. Tito was lucky to be playing with talented musicians. Many of them had written and played music for Benny Goodman and other top bandleaders. They taught Tito how to put music down on paper.

During slow times on board ship, Tito found time to practice what he was learning. He completed an **arrangement** of a tune called "El bajo de Chapotín." He mailed the new arrangement to Machito, who had his band perform the song.

In July 1944, Tito's younger sister Anna died due to a serious illness. She was only eighteen. Tito was given emergency leave from the navy to attend her funeral. Shortly after the funeral, Tito took his parents to a nearby music club. People asked him to play the piano. He sat down and played two beautiful songs. The first was to honor Anna's memory. The second was dedicated to his mother.

This photograph shows sailors doing exercises aboard the U.S.S. Santee in 1942.

Home Again

Tito was discharged from the navy several months later. His life had another change in store in him. In December 1944, Tito married Milta Sanchez. Three years later, their son Ronald was born. Two more children, Tito Jr. and their daughter Audrey, were born in 1970 and 1971. The marriage ended in divorce, probably because Tito's work took him away from home so much.

Tito was in his early twenties and eager to learn everything he could about music. The government paid for **veterans** to get an education on the G.I. Bill. *G.I.* is a slang term for soldier.

Entrance requirements were relaxed at many colleges so **veterans** like Tito who had not graduated from high school could get in.

Tito attended the Juilliard School of Music in New York City from 1945 to 1947. He learned new skills and improved on what he already knew. At Juilliard, he learned to write musical scores for movies and how to lead an orchestra. Outside of school, Tito learned to play another instrument that was becoming popular among young musicians—the vibraphone.

A vibraphone (also called vibes) is a **percussion** instrument that resembles the xylophone. The difference is that the vibraphone has metal bars instead of wooden ones like the xylophone. Metal produces a sharp, clear sound in contrast to the denser, more rounded sound of wooden bars. The vibraphone also has a special device to create a longer tone, or vibration, when the bars are struck.

A Rich Musical Life

These were busy, happy times. For the next two years, Tito played with different bands or orchestras while he went to school. He played with his old friend José Curbelo again. A new type of music called the **mambo** was influencing New York musicians. It combined the sounds of **swing** with **Latin music.** It was fun to dance to.

The Juilliard School of Music was housed in this building while Tito attended classes there.

In September of 1947, Tito joined an orchestra led by Pupi Campo. Tito was the drummer and musical director. Here, Tito met trumpet player Jimmy Frisaura, an experienced musician who had played with many big bands. The two became close friends. When Tito formed his own bands later on, Frisaura joined him. He played with Tito for over forty years until his death in 1998.

Tito also began to collaborate, or work together, with a piano player in Pupi Campo's orchestra named José Esteves Jr., who was known as Joe Loco. Like Tito, Joe was a talented **composer** and **arranger.** They worked on several arrangements for Campo's orchestra. Tito was working with a group that was becoming one of the top Latin bands.

This is a picture of Tito playing drums during the 1950s.

Chapter 4:
Swinging with the Mambo King

During the summer of 1948, the Pupi Campo Orchestra was playing a club in New York City. Federico Pagani, a dance promoter, came to listen. A dance promoter is a person who finds bands to play at dances. When the band took a short break, Pagani saw Tito teaching a new song he was working on to Joe Loco and the other musicians.

Pagani listened as Tito played a phrase on the piano and sang a melody for them. After the break, the orchestra played a haunting new melody for the audience. Its beauty made Pagani break out in goose bumps. Afterwards, the dance promoter asked Tito the name of the tune. Tito replied, "I haven't titled it yet. *Es un picadillo.*" (Spanish for "It's a mish mash"). Tito recorded the song later that year under the title "Picadillo."

Pagani was impressed with Tito's talent. He invited Tito to play at the nearby Alma Dance Studio. Tito accepted. He asked several musicians from the Pupi Campo Orchestra to play with him for the one-time-only afternoon performance. Pagani called the group The Picadilly Boys. Dancers loved their sound. For weeks afterward, people talked about the great music they heard that one afternoon.

The following spring, Tito left Pupi Campo's band. At twenty-six, he was ready to strike out on his own as leader of The Picadilly Boys. Jimmy Frisaura and other members of Campo's band went with him.

The Palladium Ballroom

Latin music, especially the **mambo,** was very popular during the late 1940s through the 1950s. The mambo referred to both the music and the dance. The dance is a partner dance with a series of tight moves back and forth as the hips move. People flocked to places it was played. In the early 1950s, the Palladium Ballroom in New York City was called The Home of the Mambo.

Shortly after Tito left the Pupi Campo Orchestra, he became a major attraction at the Palladium. His orchestra, and those of Machito and Tito Rodríguez (a friend from Tito's high school years) played mambo music to large crowds. There was an air of excitement each night. The tables nearest the stage filled with movie stars and other famous people.

People pressed against one another to watch the dancing and look at the stars. Dance studios often sent their students to watch and learn from the great mambo dancers.

Tito played with such tremendous energy that his drumsticks often broke into splinters during his drum **solos.** The crowd went wild. Sometimes the dance floor rippled with movement. Tito, who enjoyed dancing himself, loved that others had such a wonderful time, too.

The Palladium Ballroom became the place to hear the most modern of Latin sounds. **Jazz** musicians dropped in to listen to the **mambo** during their breaks from playing music at nearby clubs. Soon, jazz musicians were blending the mambo sound into their music.

The Two Titos

Pablo "Tito" Rodríguez and Tito Puente had known each other since 1939. As teenagers, they had lived a few doors away from each other in Spanish Harlem. In addition to being Puerto Rican, the two Titos shared an interest in Latin music. They became friends. As adults, both led Latin bands that influenced popular music in the late 1940s and 1950s. As an adult, Pablo would also be known by the nickname Tito. In 1949 Rodríguez hired Puente to **arrange** some songs for a record he was making.

The **mambo** had a positive effect on the people who came to listen and dance. **Discrimination** against nonwhites seemed to melt away. **Latinos,** African Americans, Jews, Irish, and Italians all came together at the Palladium to listen to the exciting new music and dance the mambo.

Tito's Orchestra

Tito was getting closer to national fame. His first major hit was a song called "Abaniquito." People all over the country heard it on the radio and loved it.

The more success he had, the harder Tito worked. His orchestra played Latin versions of popular **jazz** songs, and they played mambos with a **swing** influence. Tito did the **arrangements** of these songs for every instrument in his orchestra— four trumpets, three trombones, four saxophones, and a **rhythm** section that included a piano, bass, timbales, congas, and bongos.

People were entertained by Tito's facial expressions.

At twenty-seven, Tito was turning out record after record with the word mambo in it—*Tito Puente y Los Diablos del Mambo* ("Tito Puente and the Devils of the Mambo") and *Tito Puente and his Mambo Boys.* One night a few years later, Tito played several musical arrangements live on New York radio. His songs "Ran Kan Kan," "Mambo City," and "Mambo Inn" won over more listeners. These songs gave rise to Tito's musical nickname—*El Rey del Mambo* ("The King of the Mambo").

In 1952 the Palladium Dance Hall only hired bands that played the mambo. Two years later, the mambo craze had reached its peak. A show called "The Mambo-Rhumba Festival" went on a successful national tour. The show played in 56 cities across the United States and featured several bands. The bands of Tito Puente, Pupi Campo, and Joe Loco played. For the first time, musicians of color—Latinos and African Americans—were being paid more than other bands.

This is the cover of one of Tito's many albums.

Tito Puente admired the talent of percussionist Mongo Santamaria.

Chapter 5
Making Music…and More

Tito's career soared during the 1950s. His orchestra now included two **percussionists**: conga player Mongo Santamaria and bongo player Willie Bobo. Both would later have successful bands of their own. Throughout the years, Tito played with many musicians and singers whose talents he admired.

In 1955 Tito recorded *Puente in Percussion* with his new percussion players. This album was a creative landmark. The album was unusual because it used only percussion and bass instruments. Bass instruments are instruments having the lowest-pitched sounds. There were no horns or piano to play melody. The album was modeled after the drumming used in a religious tradition called *santería*. Tito had become interested in the tradition because of its ties to Cuba.

Santería had roots in Africa and Cuba. In Africa, drums had been used for centuries not only to communicate between tribes,

Sheila E.

Sheila E. is a popular percussionist who was born in 1957 in Oakland, California. When she was only three, Sheila played with the family's percussion instruments. Her father, Pete Escovedo, was leader of a **Latin jazz** band. Sheila often went to his band rehearsals. When she was only five, her father invited her onstage to play a drum **solo** in front of 3,000 people. The audience loved her. Sheila had fun. She told her father that when she grew up, she wanted to play drums.

Whenever he came to town, Tito Puente visited Sheila's family and often stayed for dinner. Sheila called him Uncle Tito. She said of him, "He was as charming as royalty and his smile would light the darkest day." Sheila remembers listening to *Puente in Percussion,* one of her favorite albums, when she was six.

In 1971, when Sheila was fourteen years old, Tito invited her to sit in with him and his orchestra. Sheila also played with her father's band before she became a solo artist in 1984. She was the opening act for Prince on his 1984–1985 tour. Around this time Sheila had a few hits and could often be seen on MTV. In 1989 Sheila, her father, her brother Juan, and Tito Puente made an hour-long music video titled *La Familia* ("Family"). It features Sheila, Pete Escovedo, and Tito drumming together.

but also in tribal religious dances. African drumming tradition made its way to Cuba when enslaved Africans were brought to the Americas.

*Puente in **Percussion*** was not a major success, but it brought the Afro-Cuban drumming tradition to the attention of the modern world. Years later, Tito's album would influence a young drummer and family friend named Sheila E.

Building Musical Bridges

Tito recorded two albums in 1956 that drew attention. *Cuban Carnival* was his first widely successful album. Two of its songs became big hits. People loved "Pa' los rumberos" and "Que será mi china" so much that they became classics. "Pa' los rumberos" would be recorded sixteen years later by a **Latino** musician named Carlos Santana. Another album, *Puente Goes **Jazz,*** was released a few months after *Cuban Carnival.* It featured Tito's **arrangements** of several jazz classics.

The following year, the Cuban government honored great Cuban musicians of the past fifty years in a special ceremony. Tito's Cuban friend Mario Bauzá made sure Tito was formally recognized for bringing people of all backgrounds together with his Cuban-influenced music. Tito was the only nonCuban to be honored.

Shortly after this honor, Tito recorded the most successful album of his career. *Dance Mania* exploded onto the music scene in 1958 and remained popular for years afterwards. The album featured several different Latin dance **rhythms,** including the **mambo** and the cha-cha. People around the world loved dancing to the upbeat songs with their distinctive rhythms. "El Cayuco" became an immediate hit with the public. Several other songs became classics, including "Hong Kong Mambo."

Tito rode the wave of his national popularity. He recorded over thirty albums in the 1950s. He wrote original songs and did **arrangements** of other tunes. Tito had a talent for creating his own sound by making a few changes here and there to other people's songs. Crowds at the Palladium were treated to something new almost every week.

Branching Out

In 1960 Tito recorded an album called *Revolving Bandstand*. He put two big bands in the recording studio. One band had a Latin **rhythm** section. The other had a **jazz** rhythm section. First, the jazz band would play a jazz tune. Then the Latin band would play the bridge of the tune in Latin style. A bridge is a musical passage that links two sections of a song together. The jazz and Latin bands traded off throughout each song. Using the two kinds of music in separate parts of the same song was an unusual, yet interesting, way to play a song.

Revolving Bandstand was not released until the 1970s. The people who decided what music to release for the record company did not have a good understanding of Tito's music. They wanted to release albums that would sell a lot of copies. Tito's music was unusual and interesting, but not all of his records were popular. There were hundreds of Tito's songs that the new record company never released because many of them did not fit the popular style that sold a lot of albums.

During the 1960s Tito's music started to attract attention in other countries. In 1962 Tito went on his first concert tour to Japan, where **Latin music** was starting to gain an audience. Tito helped make Latin music popular there. After his first successful tour in 1962, he returned to Japan several times to play for many enthusiastic fans.

The Palladium Ballroom closed its doors in 1966, ending the golden era of the mambo. Tito's style of Latin music had been at its peak in the 1950s. Then it lost its appeal with younger listeners.

Tito's music was not as popular, but it was still in demand enough that he toured frequently. He continued to perform and record. He encouraged the work of female Latin singers and recorded with Celia Cruz and La Lupe. Both women were extraordinary singers and performers.

This photograph shows Tito Puente marching in New York City's Puerto Rican Day Parade in 1999.

Tito stepped outside his role as a bandleader of **Latin music** to try other things. In 1967 Tito performed in concert at the Metropolitan Opera in New York. Tito **conducted** a symphony orchestra that played his music. The concert added to Tito's reputation as a talented **composer.**

Tito hosted his own television program on a Spanish-language network in the late 1960s. It was called *El Mundo de Tito Puente* ("The World of Tito Puente"). In 1968 Tito led the Puerto Rican Day parade in New York City. The next year, the mayor of New York presented Tito with a key to the city. When a person is given a key to a city, it means the person has done something that honors the city. Tito's success made Puerto Ricans and Cubans proud.

Celia Cruz (1929–2003)

Celia Cruz was called The Queen of Latin Music. One of Cuba's most famous singers, she was known for her deep, powerful voice. Tito described the effect her voice had on him the first time he heard her on the radio: "It was powerful and energetic. I swore it was a man. I'd never heard a woman sing like that."

 Cruz was born in Havana, Cuba. She studied voice and music theory at the Conservatory of Music in Havana and began singing on the radio and in small clubs. In 1949 she toured Mexico and Venezuela with a band. The next year, she joined La Sonora Matancera, one of Cuba's most popular bands. They were often on TV and radio. They went on tours and appeared in several films produced in Mexico. During the 1950s Cruz sang at Havana's famous Tropicana nightclub.

Cruz moved to the United States in 1960. She played with Tito Puente and recorded twenty records during the 1960s. Young **Latinos** discovered Cruz when **salsa** became popular in the 1970s.

Cruz was famous for wearing colorful costumes that had feathers, sequins, and lace. She won the Latin **Grammy** award for Best Salsa Performance in 2000. She recorded more than 70 albums before her death in 2003.

When Tito Puente played, his concentration was total. This is a picture of Tito playing at the Palladium Ballroom in the 1960s.

Chapter 6:
Still Going Strong

In the late 1960s, **Latin music** began to change. Musicians all over the United States began to experiment with combining different musical styles. In New York, Latin music still had a strong base of support among musicians and their audiences. A musical style called **salsa** became popular.

Salsa is a broad term for the Latin music that became popular in the 1960s. It includes many kinds of Latin music, such as the **mambo,** the cha-cha, and other types of Caribbean music. Tito played this updated version of Afro-Cuban music. It borrowed characteristics from other musical styles as well, including **jazz,** rock, and **rhythm and blues.**

Musical Hit

In the early 1970s, a young **Latino** rock musician named Carlos Santana introduced Tito's music to a new generation of listeners. Santana included his version of Tito's song "Oye Como Va" on his 1970 *Abraxas* album. Santana's version of this song Tito had recorded in 1962 became an instant hit with rock fans. Soon Santana's version was an international hit. It was popular with **Latinos** all over the world. "Oye Como Va" is still played on rock radio stations.

Tito did not mind too much when people would ask him at a show to play "Santana's song." His attitude was that Santana was exposing more people to **Latin music.** That was always a good thing, in Tito's opinion.

Carlos Santana used his electric guitar to introduce a new generation of listeners to Latin music.

Santana recorded another song of Tito's in 1972. It also became a big hit for him. "Pa' los rumberos" was from Tito's 1956 *Cuban Carnival* album. Tito liked Santana's rock-flavored version of the song. He included some of Santana's changes into his own performances of the song.

The two artists appeared together in concert for the first time in 1977. Their bands played at the Roseland Ballroom in New York. People who had never seen Tito play before were amazed at how he played drums and **conducted** his orchestra at the same time.

Carlos Santana

Guitar player Carlos Santana introduced a new generation to Latin sounds in the 1970s. Born in Mexico in 1947, his family moved to San Francisco, California, when he was fifteen. His father taught him to play violin. When Santana was eight, he switched to guitar.

Santana's group combined rock with Latin-style **percussion.** The band's second album, *Abraxas,* became a number one record in 1970. One of the songs, "Oye Como Va," became an international hit. It was originally recorded by Tito Puente.

In 1998 Santana's group was voted into the Rock and Roll Hall of Fame. In 1999 Carlos Santana released the album *Supernatural.* It sold more than 20 million copies and received eight **Grammy** awards.

A newspaper writer who attended the concert said it was a great show: "Puente **conducted** his fifteen-piece orchestra with snaps of his head and sweeps of his hands while playing timbales; at one point, when he signaled with his trademark stick over the head gesture, the entire brass section, spread in a row along his left, rose as one and played. Folks went wild."

Latin Percussion

Interest in **Latin music** grew again in the 1970s, both in the United States and in other countries. A man named Martin Cohen formed a company called Latin **Percussion.** They made Latin percussion instruments and sold them worldwide. To bring attention to the instruments, Cohen put together a group of Latin musicians to tour Europe and Japan.

Tito was one of Cohen's musical heroes. Cohen was thrilled when Tito agreed to go on tour with the small band that Cohen called the LP **Jazz** Ensemble (*LP* stood for "Latin Percussion"). Audiences everywhere loved them. Tito began to realize how popular his music was worldwide.

Cohen got to know Tito better as he traveled with the band. Tito's musical talent and outgoing personality won him over. He said that Tito was "a constant source of inspiration" who kept him smiling with his sense of humor and quick replies.

More Success

Tito won his first **Grammy** award in 1979. The award was for his album *Homenaje a Beny* (Homage to Benny). The album featured his large orchestra and several singers, including his longtime friend, Celia Cruz.

True to his nature, Tito was generous in giving credit and praise to fellow musicians he worked with. He described Cruz as the queen of Latin music and pointed out that people loved her singing "because she's so beautiful."

Tito was also generous with his time. When he performed at colleges around the United States, Tito worked with young musicians who came to learn from him. In 1980 Tito and a group of musicians set up a music scholarship fund in his name at Juilliard, where Tito had gone to school after World War II. The fund would help gifted young musicians further their studies.

Tito believed it was important for young Latin percussionists to be able to read music. Then when they went into a recording studio, they would know what they were doing. Tito explained, "It's not only what you learn in the streets. You've really got to go and study."

Grammy Awards

The Grammy Award is a recording industry award that is presented every year by the Recording Academy. It is given to honor excellence in the recording arts and sciences. The award is given to musicians as well as those who help record the music. Some Grammy awards are given to honor

special achievements in the recording industry. The Tech Award honors individuals or companies who have made contributions of outstanding technical importance to the recording field. The Lifetime Achievement Award honors an artist's accomplishments over a lifetime of work. The 2003 award went to Tito Puente after his death.

The Latin Grammy Awards were started in 2000 to honor artistic achievement in the field of **Latin music.** The show was the first prime-time television show (a program broadcast in the evening hours when the audience is the largest) that was mostly in Spanish and Portuguese. Audiences all over the world watched the awards show.

A New Direction

In the early 1980s, Tito signed a recording contract with Concord Records, a company that focused mostly on **jazz** recordings. Tito changed the name of the LP Jazz Ensemble to Tito Puente **Latin Jazz** Ensemble (later called Tito Puente and His Latin Ensemble).

Tito won his second **Grammy** award in 1983 for the record *On Broadway*. It was his first recording for the new company.

The success of *On Broadway* took Tito in another direction. Up to this time, Latin jazz had not received the major commercial success that other musical styles like rock music had. With the release of *On Broadway*, Latin jazz began to receive more attention from listeners and the recording industry.

Tito's records throughout the 1980s were marked by refreshing, creative **arrangements** of his own tunes and the tunes of other artists. In 1984 Tito named his second album for Concord Records *El Rey*, after one of his nicknames. The album included new arrangements of popular jazz classics and a remake of Tito's popular song "Oye Como Va."

Tito was honored repeatedly for his musical talent. He won a third Grammy award for **Mambo** *Diablo* in 1985. In 1987 he was voted top **percussionist** in a reader's poll taken by *Downbeat*, one of the most respected jazz magazines. That same year, Tito won an award called the Eubie. It was given to him by the National Academy of Recording Arts and Sciences to recognize his more than fifty years of making important contributions to music.

One of the many honors Tito Puente received for his work was a star on the Hollywood Walk of Fame in 1990.

Chapter 7:
A Star to the End

In 1993 Tito began a new stage in his personal life. He married Margie Ascencio. He kept his usual busy schedule in his professional life. Sometimes he would talk about slowing down, but he never did. Throughout the early 1990s, Tito performed worldwide, playing up to 30 **jazz** festivals a year. He also played other concerts, dances, and club dates. He once told a friend as a joke that his main ambition was to be in the first band to play on the moon.

Tito worked on a variety of projects. He made guest appearances on television shows. He became friends with actor and comedian Bill Cosby after appearing on *The Cosby Show*. He also appeared as a guest on late night talk shows and *Sesame Street*. His voice and music were also featured on *The Simpsons*. On this show, he was hired to be a music instructor for Lisa's band class.

Tito worked in movies. He recorded sound tracks for films such as *Zoot Suit*. Tito wrote and performed the music in the 1992 movie *Mambo King*. He also appeared as himself in the film. The movie is about **Latin music** at the Palladium Ballroom in New York. He also performed the movie's title song at the **Grammy** Awards that year, along with other well-known Latin music artists.

Mambo King, released in 1991, marked an important achievement. It was Tito's 100th album. He became one of only a handful of artists ever to record that many albums. Tito dedicated the album to his old friend Jimmy Frisaura, who was ill and unable to record with him.

Leading the Way

Tito supported the efforts of younger musicians by appearing as a special guest on their albums. He saw himself as a role model for young people. He considered younger musicians to be the new interpreters of the Latin music tradition. Young **Latinos,** in turn, looked up to him as someone to learn from. They saw how his music reflected a positive, energetic side of Latin **culture** that brought happiness to people.

Tito made a recording and a video, both titled *La Familia* ("Family"), with **percussionists** Sheila E. and her father Pete Escovedo. In the video, viewers can see the joy music brought to Tito. Escovedo introduced Tito as Sheila's Uncle Tito—not because he really was, but because of the affection they all felt for each other.

Tito Puente with his son Tito Puente Jr. Like his father, Tito Jr. studied the piano, wrote music, and played in New York City clubs at a young age. He wrote the song "Caliente" (Spanish for "hot" or "fiery") as a tribute to his father.

More Honors

During his lifetime, Tito earned dozens of awards and honors. It seemed whatever Tito did, people loved his work. Hollywood honored the tireless performer with a star on the Hollywood Walk of Fame in 1990. That same year, Tito won a fourth **Grammy** Award for the song "Lambada Timbales."

Tito performed for presidents and was honored as a "Living Legend" by the United States Library of Congress. In 1993 an all-star **jazz** orchestra played a tribute to Tito at Carnegie Hall in New York City. In 1997 Tito was given the National Medal of the Arts. He went to the White House to receive it.

By 1998 Tito had recorded 116 albums, written over 450 songs, and created more than 2,000 **arrangements.** The following year, Tito won the Latin Grammy for Best Traditional Tropical Performance for the album **Mambo** *Birdland*. The Latin Grammy Awards were created in 2000 to recognize Latin artists. The awards were broadcast mainly in Spanish on network television.

Tito led his own bands for over fifty years. He continued to make music until just before he died on May 31, 2000, after undergoing heart surgery. He was 77 years old. Musical knowledge, natural ability, creativity, and hard work were the secrets to Tito's long career. His music brought people of all ages, races, and

Tito's children, Tito Puente Jr. and Audrey Puente, accepted Tito's Latin Grammy award for Mambo Birdland *in 2000.*

cultures together. Tito's music lives on wherever **Latin jazz** sounds inspire new generations of musicians. Today, *El Rey's* son, Tito Puente Jr., carries on the tradition of his father. He makes and performs **Latin music.**

Glossary

arrange   change a piece of music for voices or instruments other than those for which it was originally written

barrio   Spanish-speaking part of a city or town

bilingual   person who speaks two languages

composer   person who writes music

conduct   lead a group of musicians as they play a song

culture   way a group of people live, such as the food they eat, the clothes they wear, and the values and beliefs they share

discrimination   unfair treatment of people based on their race or other characteristic

ethnic   about a large group of people that have a background based on common characteristics such as race, religion, language, or nationality

Grammy   recognition given in the United States music industry

improvise   in jazz, the action of making up and playing music on the spot

integrated   not separated by race

jazz   form of music based on improvisation, solos, and changing rhythms. It was developed by African Americans in the early 20th century.

Latin music   music that first came from Latin America. Also, any music played with Latin sounds—either traditional or modern.

Latin jazz   blending of Latin music with jazz that is also called salsa or Afro-Cuban music

Latino   person from Latin America or one whose ancestors came from Latin America

mambo   fast form of Latin dance music that is a mixture of African, Cuban, and jazz. It also is the dance people do as they listen to this music

percussion   instruments played by striking or beating, such as drums, bongos, and xylophones

rhythm   steady beat in a piece of music

rhythm and blues   form of fast dance music developed by African Americans in cities. Rhythm and blues includes drums, piano, bass, and electric guitar.

salsa   swinging Latin music with a mix of Cuban, Puerto Rican, and jazz elements

solo   in jazz, part of a song featuring one musician

swing   kind of jazz music popular in the 1940s and 1950s that people enjoyed dancing to

veteran   person who has fought in a war

Timeline

1923: Tito Puente is born in New York City on April 20.

1935: Becomes member of the "Stars of the Future" at his church.

1939: Drops out of school to become a full-time musician.

1941: Makes his recording debut with Vincent's López's Suave Swing Orchestra and appears in film shorts.

1942: Joins Machito's orchestra on timbales; drafted into the navy.

1945–1947: Studies at Juilliard School of Music and works with several bands. Becomes drummer and musical director of the Pupi Campo Orchestra.

1948: Leads his own group, The Picadilly Boys.

1949: Becomes a full-time bandleader, leading ensembles for the next 51 years of his life. Has his first hit song with "Abaniquito."

1955: Records one of his most creative albums, *Puente in Percussion,* using percussion and bass only.

1957: Cuban government formally recognizes Puente in a ceremony honoring great Cuban musicians of previous fifty years, the only non-Cuban so honored.

1962: Begins to be known internationally. Records "Oye Como Va" which becomes a big hit for Carlos Santana eight years later.

1967: Presents a concert of his own compositions at the Metropolitan Opera in New York.

1979: Tours Japan with the LP (Latin Percussion) Jazz Ensemble and wins his first Grammy award.

1980: Establishes scholarship fund for young musicians.

1991: Celebrates the release of his 100th album.

1997: Receives the National Medal of the Arts from President Clinton at the White House.

2000: Tito Puente dies of heart failure.

Further Information

Further reading

Flanders, Julian, Ed. *The Story of Music: Gospel, Blues, and Jazz. Volume 5.* Danbury, Conn: Grolier Educational, 2001.

Martin, Marvin. *Extraordinary People in Jazz.* New York: Children's Press, 2003.

Vigna, Guiseppe. *Jazz and Its History.* Hauppauge, NY: Barron's Educational Series, Inc., 1999.

Addresses

The Tito Puente Scholarship Fund
for Latino Outreach
Hackley School
293 Benedict Avenue
Tarrytown, NY 10591

UCLA Ethnomusicology Dept.
University of California
at Los Angeles
Box 951657, 2649SMB
Los Angeles, California 90095-1657

Smithsonian Jazz
Masterworks Orchestra
National Museum
of American History
Division of Cultural History
MRC 616
14th Street and Constitution
Avenue, N.W.
Washington, D.C. 20560-0616

The Children's Music Network
P.O. Box 1341
Evanston, IL 60204-1341

Index